# SPARE US!

# SPARE US!

## A HARRODY

with Bruno Vincent

abacus
books

ABACUS

First published in Great Britain in 2023 by Abacus

5 7 9 10 8 6

Copyright © A Harrody (Bruno Vincent), 2023
Illustrations by Emanuel Santos

The moral right of the author has been asserted.

A CIP catalogue record for this book is
available from the British Library.

ISBN 978-0-349-14606-5

Typeset in Garamond by M Rules
Printed and bound in Great Britain by Clays Ltd, Elcograf S.p.A.

Papers used by Abacus are from well-managed forests
and other responsible sources.

MIX
Paper from
responsible sources
FSC® C104740

Abacus
An imprint of
Little, Brown Book Group
Carmelite House
50 Victoria Embankment
London EC4Y 0DZ

An Hachette UK Company
www.hachette.co.uk

www.littlebrown.co.uk

*Do not begin your book with a serious quotation, it doesn't make you sound more clever*

Julius Caesar

# Chapter 1

It was a bitterly cold day, and a breeze as stiff as one of my father's smiles was gusting along between the tombstones.

I wished I had worn something warmer. I was waiting for my father and brother to appear in the royal cemetery for a crisis meeting, owing to my recent announcement that I would be moving to America.

Grey clouds scurried across the sky and I shivered in my thin shirt. As I stood there, I wondered whether the dead were still around us, looking on with an approving smile or a concerned frown? Just imagine them standing next to you. Henry VIII. Queen Victoria. Ken Dodd. Lenin.

Being in places like this always made me philosophical.

I cast my eye over the marble mausoleums, covered with ivy and moss. Just as I was thinking about crumbling, outdated relics, my father appeared. Willy was by his side.

Distracting us from what was really on our minds, Pa delivered one of his impromptu history lectures, pointing out architectural details and getting specific about the dead folk under our feet. But postponing the inevitable just made Willy and me even more tense.

When at last conversation turned to the matter at hand, I could tell at once they were both furious.

I tried to explain myself, but they wouldn't listen.

I kept starting to speak, but they talked over me.

I was desperate. I had nothing but love for my cowardly, selfish father and my balding, violent, self-righteous brother. I would never do anything to cast them in a bad light.

Yet it soon seemed that they didn't even understand why I was leaving.

Really?

I was aghast.

After everything that had happened, how could they feel an explanation was still needed? It amazed me.

All I had ever wanted was privacy.

In order to get it, it seemed that an exceptionally detailed 500,000-word book was in order . . .

# Chapter 2

There was a lot about my childhood that was idyllic.

For instance, the exclusive Ladgrove school, tucked away in the English countryside, which I attended as a boy.

It was a luxurious private school with a deep history, surrounded by ancient woodlands, where boys dwelt among tottering castellated turrets and brick chimneys, viewing the outside world through rose-tinted windows set within the crumbling gothic masonry.

There were lavish platters of sweets and chocolates on tuck days. When it was a pupil's birthday he was served his own choice of dessert with heaps of cream and lashings of custard. (Although if any of the servants were impertinent, it would not only be the custard that was lashed – an extra treat.)

I have always remembered one particular sight.

It was in the dining hall. And before you ask, we did *not* all receive our post via personalised owls! In fact, our letters were delivered in the normal way, on silver plates by a footman.

(Although I remember that an owl once got into the main chamber while we were eating tiffin, and had to be shot with an iron crossbow bequeathed to the school for the very purpose in Geoffrey Chaucer's will.)

No, the particular memory that comes to mind was that

during luncheon when one of our masters, Sir Thomas Huge-Brownley, wanted our attention, he rang a little silver bell. How did he think this bell would be heard over two hundred hungry boys eating and yelling about the cost of Railtrack shares over their spotted dick?

But he didn't give up. He would stand there, ringing and ringing and not getting anyone's attention, becoming ever more red in the face as no one paid him the slightest heed.

I felt sorry for him. Ringing that bell, trying to stop the noise by making more and more noise. Utterly failing, and making a fool of himself into the bargain.

My therapist has asked me why this image haunts me so, and I can't quite put my finger on it.

# Chapter 3

My history teacher embarrassed me one day by asking me a question about the British royal succession. None of the other kids in the class knew the answer either, but he singled me out.

'Come on, Wales, you ought to know this! It's your own family history after all!'

I thought this was too much. My family, after all, had labelled me the 'spare' – a shadow prince, a regal auxiliary, a fleshly insurance plan no more important than any other theoretical concept.

Now, that was fine by me. You wouldn't see me complaining about that. Certainly not within the covers of a bestselling book and then also going on and on about it in interviews. No sir. That's just not me.

I'm at peace with being the 'spare'.

But to have to actually *read books* about this family who consider me superfluous? That felt like going too far, indeed.

I felt humiliated. I went up to him after class and requested that he not show me up in this way.

He bridled. He did not expect his students to speak back.

'What's this, Wales?' he said, and his enormous bushy eyebrows shot up to his hairline like two hirsute badgers subjected to examination by a cold-fingered proctologist.

'I just think it's unfair to single me out like that sir,' I said. 'It reminds other boys of the difference between us!'

He was not impressed.

I skulked away, still cross, with vague thoughts that if (heaven forbid) I ever did end up on the throne, it would be a dark day for history teachers.

But the next time he came to class he gave me a small present to make amends. It was a wooden ruler with all the monarchs of England on it, so I could remember them.

There they were, from William the Conqueror (1066–1087) to Grannie (1953–). In the space beneath I could envisage 'Pa . . . – . . .' and 'Willy . . . – . . .' being engraved in due course.

I was amazed that he had gone to the effort of creating this unique, bespoke piece of woodwork just for me. I felt obliged to put it in my pencil case.

Truce had been declared. When it came to inflexible rulers, I felt I'd experienced enough already, but here was yet another one forced upon me.

# Chapter 4

There was a mistress at school with whom I had a special relationship.

Whereas all the others were motherly and caring, she was sharp and strict. She often caught boys by the elbow and bashed their faces against the wall, just to teach them a lesson.

Whenever we were ill or got injuries on the sports field, she would stand over our beds, laughing, and poke sticks into our eyes.

She had a deformation of the spine and had to climb or descend the stairs very slowly and carefully. All the while, us boys would point and laugh at her, and pull insulting grimaces and dance around in imitation of her disability.

She had to put up with this constant abuse at our hands, and I was the worst culprit. But somehow, she knew that I meant it in jest, and even though she would inflict violent pain on me if she could manage to reach out and grab me by the collar, she mostly failed to do so.

In her heart I think she was laughing along, and really thought I was an absolutely top bloke.

How we loved her. The school really was a very warm and caring place.

# Chapter 5

Most of the staff at Ladgrove school were sultry maidens, sash-aying along the corridors and waking us boys each morning by cooing softly from the doorways, leaving trays of hot buttered scones and bowls of steaming porridge in the centre of which slowly melted scoopfuls of clotted cream.

They tended to our every need, ironing our jodhpurs, polishing our RayBans, then appearing before lights out to deliver our Horlicks surrounded in a halo of candlelight, just in time to read the closing figures from the day's FTSE share index.

They also washed our hair. We boys would lie supine in tubs while they lathered our scalps, singing songs and reciting poetry. Then they would dry us with our personally monogrammed Egyptian cotton towels.

It was a heavenly time being around these women, and naturally we all fell in love with them.

But it was perfectly natural and healthy. For boys with fraught relationships with their parents, you might have expected some serious psychological issues to have arisen.

Not for me.

I was unaffected and was as well-adjusted as any mother boy. I mean, other boy.

# Chapter 6

From Ladgrove, at twelve I went on to Eton.

Eton was a magisterial place, deliberately built so as to make little boys feel awed and overpowered when setting eyes on it. This certainly worked on me.

But worse was to come when I actually attended lessons.

Imagine my horror when I turned up to my first period of French to discover the teacher speaking *en français* from beginning to end.

'Sacré bleu! Violet Beauregarde!' I thought. 'Achtung baby!'

I went up to my teacher afterwards and said, 'Excuse me sir, I'm very sorry, but I'm afraid I'm in the wrong class.'

He didn't bat an eyelid.

'My dear boy,' he said, thankfully in Grannie's English. 'Have no fear. Every boy in this entire school is in the right class. That's all that matters. So you have nothing to worry about.'

I left feeling very reassured.

# Chapter 7

Eton was a grand place, indeed. It had been set up in the fifteenth century by my ancestor Henry VI.

He had intended it to be a place of supreme purpose and power, and had endowed it with such precious artefacts as Jesus's Crown of Thorns, a cricket bat belonging to Thomas Becket, and one of the testicles of Alexander the Great preserved in beaver's wax.

Then of course there was the humblingly illustrious roster of former pupils, who included among their number 27 prime ministers, 34 Nobel laureates, 19 Oscar winners, 6 Sultans, 3 Grand Muftis, two Doctor Whos and a Milky Bar Kid. It was quite a lot to live up to.

Every student dressed each day in full mourning for the death of Henry VI. And after all, why not – he was a truly great monarch. Taking the throne aged just nine months, spending many years in a slothful, torpid state during which he spoke not a word, allowing his French wife to take power, and letting the country slide into a destructive decades-long civil war. He was a symbol of all that was right with the monarchy.

What better personage to be remembered all these years later by wealthy youngsters dressing in expensive, outdated garb?

And yet, of course, who knows what the future might bring?

Perhaps, if things go a certain way, one day five centuries hence, pupils at a school might be dressing in mourning for me.

I wonder what that would be like.

The school at that time would probably be on Mars or even Neptune. The pupils would hopefully be sporty and keen, and play by the rules in all their games – whether it is moon cricket, intergalactic beer pong, or the very risky space strip rugby.

Don't dishonour me, future space students! Bare your space nuts with pride!

# Chapter 8

Eton was a whole new world to me, with a whole new language that I had to learn.

Apart from French, that is.

For instance, classes were called Divs. Teachers were called Beaks. Cigarettes were called chuggers.

On the sports field, 'drybobs' were those who played cricket, rugby or polo.

'Wetbobs' were boys who swam or played water polo.

'Skybobs' were those who parachuted out of biplanes into narrowly conscribed targets, or 'air polo' as we called it.

'Icebobs' were those who played curling, or the lads who annually re-enacted the 1723 Battle of St Petersburg on the frozen duckpond. It was always performed with the historical rigour for which the school is justly famous.

Boys who lost fingers or toes during the re-enactment were tended by apothecaries carrying historically appropriate remedies, and all were welcomed home afterwards to a mead-hall with a roaring fire and a jolly, rousing performance of the school song. Although this was partly to quieten the screams of the younger pupils. It was character building.

Such larks!

The sports didn't stop there.

Tennis, real tennis, royal tennis, crypto tennis, rock climbing, rock fetching, drain-the-rock-Johnsoning, fencing, walling, Ronseal quick-drying woodstaining, dressage, shirtage, underpantage, wiffwaff...

There were games we invented for ourselves with their own improvised rules, like corridor cricket, ceiling darts and Spongeblob Scarepants, where we would down whole bottles of Da Bomb hot sauce and see who was the last to make it to the toilet.

For athletic lads like me, there was a smorgasbord of activities on offer.

# Chapter 9

One minute we were all joking around with some hair clippers.

The next, I was completely bald and the floor around my feet was coated with tufts of ginger hair.

I gulped. I looked in the mirror. I gulped again.

When the story got out, it was a nationwide scandal.

*Harry the baldy, Harry the thicko, Bald-faced idiot*, the headlines said.

I couldn't believe I had been so stupid.

What had I been thinking?

I vowed never, ever, to bring the family into disrepute ever again.

# Chapter 10

It was naughty, we all knew it. But some of us boys had taken to smoking weed out of a window near the top of the school. In order not to get caught we organised ourselves with the military precision which would serve many of us well when we buzzed off into the army to accept senior officer commissions.

When it came my turn to poke my head out of the window into the night air, I experienced peace like I hadn't for years.

Perfect solitude.

Serene countryside as far as the eye could see, beneath the beaming face of the full silver moon.

This was what I needed.

Privacy. Time away from my thoughts.

All my worries dispersed in the night air.

In the lunar glow I saw a hedgehog waddling across the car-park and in that moment I knew it was a sign. A sign from the hereafter – from the universe – from heaven.

Who knew?

It was a message, I knew that for sure.

But what did it mean?

I would ponder it for years afterwards.

'Oy Harry, you selfish ginger bastard, pass the bloody joint!' shrieked a teenage voice behind me.

'Oh yes, sorry,' I said.

# Chapter 11

One of the Palace courtiers called me into his office.

'This is very serious, Harry,' he said. 'Apparently one of the papers is going to publish a story that you are smoking cannabis. Is it true?'

'Absolutely not!'

'You're sure?'

'One hundred per cent!'

'I'll deny it then.'

'It's a disgraceful, shameful lie and it makes me feel sick to think I live in a country where such falsehoods would be perpetuated,' I said.

He said I could go. He would deal with it.

I was still seething at the intrusion and hypocrisy of it, and couldn't calm down until I'd smoked six joints.

# Chapter 12

Soon it became clear that I was regarded as 'the naughty royal'.

It seemed unfair to me. After all, I had not overseen the Amritsar Massacre nor waged an opium war with China, still less created a new religion in order to get my leg over.

I'd only been moderately foolish like any schoolboy.

Nevertheless, it stuck.

And thus, as one might expect, I lived up to it and became more naughty.

Nothing seemed more enticing to me than to sneak out of Eton to go into Windsor town for a few beers with my mates, and to have an errant afternoon of skiving.

We would drink cans of lager down by the river, occasionally chasing swans, which I reckoned was okay because they all belong to Grannie anyway.

We would loll by the Thames smoking packets of Superkings – which I called Superpas.

Then we'd go to eat at Burger King, which I referred to as Burger Pa. I would pay with a fistful of Grannies.

My appetite for Whoppers remains well known to this day.

# Chapter 13

All through my teens, I was waging a war on memory. I took any method that came to hand to obliterate my painful thoughts.

Cannabis, Smirnoff Ice, rugby, I threw myself into them all. Or threw them into me.

Whole months blip out of existence as I try to recall them. Some events I cannot be sure of at all, and need historical evidence to prove they really happened.

At night my naturally rebellious spirit made me want to roam the halls of Eton and even go further afield.

Speaking of fields, next to the school was a farm. With friends, I would climb the walls and leap down into the ploughed fields where we would run amok, picking fruits and vegetables, laughing as we ran.

Eventually Farmer Maggot caught us and gave chase, yelling in anger. We all roared with laughter and took flight, rushing at top speed until, reaching the edge of his land, we tripped and found ourselves on a path.

Hearing a noise, we hid just in time as a mysterious cloaked rider approached on a black stallion. By luck this fell spirit passed by without catching us.

'It is one of the Nazgul!' said a friend. 'A rider from Mordor!'

My therapist has since told me this is a scene from *The Lord of the Rings*, and that I've got confused between actual memories and films of the era.

'It's funny you say that,' I replied. 'I've got this awful memory of thinking I was just a character in a film, a likable but goofy guy, who finds out his life is just a soap opera completely circumscribed and controlled by an evil media tycoon, with cameras peeping in at every private moment and recording him, and manufacturing from his life a total fiction enjoyed by millions at his expense.

'When I was in this dream all I wanted to do was escape and find a life for myself on my own terms. Was that a movie?'

'No, Harry,' my therapist replied. 'That was very real.'

# Chapter 14

We were on a family hunting trip in the Highlands, and I was keen to be involved.

I was with my nanny, Mrs Tiggywinkle, who got angry whenever she was accurately referred to as 'my nanny, Mrs Tiggywinkle'.

'I'm not your nanny, I'm your friend!' she would yell, merrily boxing us on our ears.

She was taking me through the ordinary wholesome rite of passage which was getting a young lad to murder his first animal. I had a rifle which I had practised with on multiple firing ranges, and had passed several safety tests to show I was ready and responsible.

Now we approached our prey.

She crouched beside me, breathing heavily.

'When you have it in your sight and think you have the shot, Harry ...' she intoned, 'don't pull the trigger, but *squeeze* it ...'

A tense, concentration-filled moment followed ...

Then there was a colossal retort and my rifle thumped back against my chest.

'You got it! You got it!' she squealed.

I couldn't believe it was really true. I gazed in wonderment.

We both approached the carcass and she dipped her fingers in the gruesome liquid and smeared my face in it. I was at one with my victim, I had undergone the most primal rite that an animal can experience – being at one with my prey, honouring it, by wearing its essence.

'Now you are a man!' said Mrs Tiggywinkle ecstatically.

Too bad that she had recently turned vegan, and all we had been hunting was a bag of tofu with a picture of a bunny taped to the outside, propped up on the estate wall. Now I had to clean the tofu juices off my hunting jacket before the real hunt could commence.

# Chapter 15

Eton happened to be located quite near to Broadmoor, the high-security psychiatric hospital.

My father stopped in to see me at school one afternoon. He had been paying a royal visit to the hospital down the road, where he had come face to face with a prisoner who firmly believed himself to be the Prince of Wales.

'Now, now,' my father had said, wagging his finger at the fellow. 'I won't have this. I'm the *real* prince, you know?'

'Fuck off, you posh dick nozzle,' came the response.

It turned out he had been admonishing a workman who was there to re-shingle the kitchen block roof, rather than the intended patient.

'Apparently it is a not uncommon delusion,' Pa pontificated, relating the story without apparent embarrassment. 'In fact, standing there looking at him – the correct patient I mean, when I finally met him – I wondered if he was not the sane one and me the madman!'

It just so happened that my father had a new haircut that day, rather different from his former look. He was wearing different clothes. He was also standing against the light, which gave him a slightly sinister appearance, and cast his features in an unaccustomed expression.

For one moment, the thought occurred to me that he really *might* have been replaced. That the person in front of me might be a madman (guilty of unspecified but surely violent crimes) who was Pa's doppelganger, having tricked my father into changing place by his criminal guile.

'Never forget, my darling boy,' this sinister figure intoned, 'that we can never know whether we are real or not real. As Hamlet himself said, I believe best paraphrased by Kierkegaard …'

Pa being notoriously prone to pompous lectures, my fears were put at rest by the tedious forty-minute speech that followed.

# Chapter 16

Pa confessed to me that he had had an awful time at school.

He hinted at true darkness in the times he had endured at Gordonstoun where he had been sent to 'toughen up'.

Fifty years later, he still owned the teddy bear which had been his only solace in the cold stone dormitories of that dismal Scottish castle. I was truly sorry that he had suffered such merciless cruelty.

The teddy seemed to have suffered just as much. With its stuffing falling out, and rips and snags in its fabric, it represented the personality he had been left with after the savaging he had received.

Willy and I knew that Pa needed a long-term companion that was better than a scraggy old teddy covered in holes. So we were glad when he said he wanted to be together with Camilla.

We wanted him to be happy.

'Only promise us one thing,' we both urged. 'Don't marry her. It would be too much. Please don't marry.'

Camilla was pleasantness itself to our faces, when we met.

But soon afterwards, it became clear that she was leaking stories to the press to make herself look good and to place Willy and me at a disadvantage, in order to secure her future within the royal family. And, in due course, gain queenhood.

Willy and I were dismayed to realise that, in reality, Pa had swapped one leaky life companion for another.

It was with some justice that, in royal circles, Camilla quickly earned the nickname of the Golden Colander.

# Chapter 17

We had stalked the noble beast for three miles, until just at sundown it broke cover on a spur of rock.

The stag stood handsome and majestic against the fading sunlight.

I wondered what it might be thinking about. The loneliness of the highland moors, the encroachment of human development into its natural habitat. Perhaps glimpsing in the vanishing rays of Caledonian sunshine some precious ancestral memory, a beloved relative it longed to lay eyes upon once again, perhaps . . .

'Shoot the buggahhh!' muttered Pa irritably. 'I never had such an easy shot when I was your age!'

I pulled – or rather *squeezed* – the trigger.

A sharp thunderclap rang out between the highland peaks.

The noble stag remained motionless, then seemed to kneel down and lie on the rock. When we caught up to him, he was dead.

'Right between the eyes!' said the tracker.

He slashed a wound in the dead creature's belly and shoved my face in. And rubbed it around in there until I thought I would be sick, and then until I was too terrified to be sick.

Then he tore the creature's heart out, ripped a hole in it with his fingers and placed it on my head like a cap – an essential part of the ceremony.

These deer were not callously murdered, but carefully culled in order to help keep the deer population in check so the local ecosystem would be preserved. I knew this full well.

At last the beast's lungs were carved out and placed on my feet to wear as shoes, and its eyeballs were dangled around my neck to ward against evil spirits. Having gone through the same ritual all my male relatives had before me, I could return to the family hold with full approval.

After all the strange and unnatural things that had happened over the preceding few years it felt like a blessing to be going through something completely normal again.

Watching while a family friend disembowelled the deer and trailed its innards over the heath, then snipping off its cock and balls for a memento, it amazed me at such times to think that outsiders considered our family a cold-blooded eccentric cult focused on cruelty and death.

# Chapter 18

I knew I didn't want to go to university. When he heard this, Pa was relieved.

'University's not for you, Harry,' he said.

My tutor at Eton agreed heartily.

'You're not a bookish lad, and that's fine,' he said.

'Gosh, no! There's nowhere I'd less rather be than a rotten old library. Books put me to sleep. I mean, like, total yawnsville!'

'Nevertheless, as a royal there's a good chance that one day you'll be requested to write a book on some subject or other close to your heart,' my tutor reflected.

At this moment shafts of golden sunshine were blazing through the ornate windows, alighting on the Eton master's coiffed silver locks. He fluffed out his gown, which bloomed with slow grace like the sail of a dhow upon the waters of the Nile catching the first ominous breath of a sirocco – the desert wind.

'If this occurs, the chances are you will have to work with a ghost writer,' quoth the pedagogue, his features shifting contemplatively so that he took on a majestic cast, half Rembrandt self-portrait, half ponderous Agamemnon dispensing fatherly advice to impetuous Achilles.

'When the time comes, try not to pick one who overwrites like a bloody ponce and makes it perfectly obvious you haven't written a word of the book, just so he can advertise his own sorry arse for future work.'

'I shall endeavour to follow your advice assiduously, master,' I asseverated. And bowing deeply, I withdrew to play rugger on those fields of Eton whereon the Duke of Wellington famously declared the Battle of Waterloo had been won.

Little did I know that my own Battle of Waterloo lay in the future. And in this case, Napoleon would come in the form of betrayal from within my own family.

# Chapter 19

I got a call from someone in the Palace.

'There's a story about to break,' they said. 'About you taking cocaine, Harry. Is it true?'

'My god! Really? You would ask me that? Really?'

'You mean it's not true?'

'I am completely revolted by the insinuation!' I said. 'The very thought! How do these abhorrent scandalmongers get away with peddling this rubbish?'

'Okay then, I'll deny it.'

I thanked him.

I was utterly dejected at my treatment by the press. In fact, so much so, that I decided a little line was in order, just to take the edge off.

# Chapter 20

Pa took me on a royal trip to South Africa.

We were to appear in public alongside Nelson Mandela and the Spice Girls. Many people were overawed to find themselves in front of such majesty and humanity, and became speechless when coming face to face with the most adored, most worshipped presence on the planet.

Of course, I had been around famous people all my life. So I took meeting the Spice Girls in my stride.

They were remorselessly upbeat, happy, positive and outgoing. 'Spice up your life!' they sang.

But I did not want to spice up my life.

My life was already a vindaloo. I wanted it to be a korma, a passanda – or even better, an omelette and chips. Sorry, Mr curry house waiter, vindaloo? It's just not my thing. And also sorry for all the historical nicking your country stuff too while we're about it.

Little did I know that in due course my life would turn from a vindaloo to a phal. (A phal is the curry that's hotter than a vindaloo.)

And I would find that *phal* from ideal. And I would suffer a *phal* from grace. My temperature would rise so much I would need a *phal*mometer. (Please cut this bit Harry – ed.)

# Chapter 21

When I heard the news, I was speechless with horror.

It seemed that my mother's former butler had published a sensational tell-all memoir, giving the inside story of his side of events, and allowing prying eyes to set foot, if prying eyes can set feet, and I imagine they might be able to, within the Palace walls.

It was disgusting.

That a trusted personage at the heart of the family should go outside and sell all the tawdry details at his disposal to the highest bidder – and then go on talk shows around the world to brag about it.

None of us could countenance the betrayal. It was unconscionable.

It was hypocrisy of the very highest order.

We were all so angry we wanted to have the man hanged, drawn and quartered. Or halved, at the very least.

In the end we had to content ourselves with knowing that the man was just an attention-seeker trying to get a few quick quid by selling his soul to the book publisher with the fattest cheque book.

The idea made my blood run cold.

# Chapter 22

It was a party to celebrate Grannie's golden jubilee.

All of the United Kingdom went wild.

There were people dancing in the street, holding block parties (which in Britain are called street parties) and congregating with ebullient joy (which in Britain involves having a cake and a cup of tea and talking to your neighbour for the first time in seven years).

There was a concert at Buckingham Palace – for one day, Buck Pal was the hippest place to be. And not just because of the number of hip replacements in action on the premises.

I sat behind Grannie as she tapped her feet and swayed along to the music. I had never loved her more, to see her vibing with the crowd in this way.

It seemed so unlike her!

After all, I wasn't sure the performers were exactly – how would one say – her cup of tea.

Then I saw she was wearing an earpiece. What a genius! She'd found a way to join in the festivities while also maintaining her own private distance.

What was *she* listening to, though?

Later, I hunted down the courtier in charge of her musical choices, and found out. I was dumbfounded to discover one of the artists playing through her earpiece – Queen – had also been on the stage in front of her!

Why had she chosen to listen to through her onePhone (as the regal mp3 player was known in the palace)? What was on the playlist for this wily septuagenarian queenster?

Then I saw.

She had only authorised artists who were members of the nobility!

Queen. Prince. Duke Ellington. Count Basie. Gladys Knight. Sir Mixalot.

I nodded, I smiled, I laughed aloud.

God bless you, ma'am!

# Chapter 23

It was agreed that I would enter the army.

The training was tough, gruelling, punishing to the extreme.

We went on long marches across tough terrain, carrying weights on our back. We were forced through such extremes of endurance that we lost our sense of self, forgot who we were, and remade ourselves again.

When we fell into our bunks at night we were throbbing all over, our bodies one generalised ache.

Many dropped out, exhausted and demoralised.

I didn't.

We were forced to run for dozens upon dozens of miles. Some of the other cadets couldn't handle it. But I could run, it seemed, for ever.

What was I running from?

I didn't know.

Scratch that – I did know. I was running from everything. Or rather, scratch that again. I was running from everything I *didn't* know.

Everything and every*one*. Which included – myself.

What was I running towards?

I couldn't tell. Nothing. Oblivion. The future, whatever that held. I just knew it couldn't be more awful than my past. I ran forwards in order to make my former life vanish.

Running on empty, running for office(r). An officer and a gentleman. The loneliness of the long-distance prince. A do run run run, a do run run.

I had the runs.

And I was *scoring* runs, too. On the scoreboard of life, my batting average was going up. Was my bowling average going down? And when would I get out?

Yet I didn't want to get out. I was in, and I wanted to get further in.

I did run run run, I did run run.

# Chapter 24

There was a loud bang and the door was flung open.

Armed men in balaclavas came rushing in and surrounded us. They were screaming violently and waving their guns around.

'Kneel!' they roared.

'I'm Harry!' I said. 'Neil's that one over there!'

'ON YOUR KNEES!' they bellowed.

They tied us to chairs, beat us, played ear-splitting music – screeching violins, howling organs, smashing pumpkins – while they put us in stress positions.

Then they put bags over our heads and hammered the soles of our feet with the butts of their rifles.

It was agony. It seemed to go on for ever.

But I was determined not to crack.

They placed lit matches under our fingernails and yelled obscenities into our ears, mixed with personalised insults and deliberate misuses of grammar.

The torture took many forms and went on over many hours.

When a gag was finally pulled from my mouth and we were told that this particularly vicious session had come to an end, I felt I had to say something.

'I think some of you lads take it a bit far with these stag weekends,' I protested, pulling my shredded boxer shorts back on. 'I'm looking forward to going back to army training.'

# Chapter 25

The last stages of training before being deployed were the most difficult.

They were not the most physically challenging – that had been the forced march across Bodmin Moor in the driving rain, the last few miles of which we had performed breaststroke.

But now we had to *study*. Great hours-long lectures on the history of tactical warfare; the differing techniques of murder by aggression and by subterfuge; the multitudinous methods of torture and survival; the basics of winning and losing.

It was like my entrance exams for Eton, but worse. Like many other cadets I began to despair that this would not be for me.

Another failure by the ginger thicko prince?

The press would have a field day.

Yet there were other cadets, I knew, who had just the same problems as me. They were struggling desperately to stay awake during the punishing afternoon lectures, especially after the rigorous physical training that would precede them in the mornings.

Desperation was in the air.

And then we were taken to a cemetery and stood to attention while a solemn poem was read aloud, commemorating the dead.

It was a fine clear morning with skylarks trilling on the

easterly breeze, and a smell of fresh cut grass rising from the manicured lawns.

'Dulce et Decorum Est', the poem went.

As the last verse of the poem came to an end I risked a glance along the line of trainee soldiers. I saw at once that there was not a dry eye in the whole parade.

Whoever thought of reading the poem to us, it was a master stroke. After that we battened down the hatches, doubled down on our efforts, and pushed on through to the finish line.

Death itself was preferable to being subjected to poetry like that, ever again.

Periodically afterwards we were read poems, always with the same effect – a massive surge in perseverance by the students.

# Chapter 26

At last, my hard work bore fruit.

It was the Passing Out ceremony for the army, where every new graduate paraded in front of my grandmother.

All my family were there, including Willy, who as a new recruit was now my inferior in rank.

It was a glorious day. The marching, the brass bands, the pomp and circumstance. Britain's proud military on parade.

When it was my turn to stand in front of Grannie, she nodded and gave a tiny smile with the corner of her mouth. I was overcome with joy, as this was the most generous emotional gesture I had ever received from her.

I had done something right for once.

I had graduated.

It was not my first Passing Out. Nor would it be my last.

# Chapter 27

After a long wait, I had finally been deployed overseas for active combat.

I got out of the royal car onto the airway tarmac and bade farewell to my bodyguards.

This was it – for the first time in my entire life I would be without my personalised armed guard. Stepping forth, alone in the world.

It was quite a forbidding moment. I felt exposed like never before, as I climbed up onto the cargo plane that would be transporting me.

From now on there would only be the combined firepower of the entire British military to protect me, as well as seventy thousand trained and heavily armed troops.

It was like being naked.

I crossed my fingers.

# Chapter 28

My first tour in Afghanistan was a whirlwind.

I was flying. F7s, F11s, F9s . . .

I was using all the keys on the computer keyboard.

The military engineering and machinery on display was awesome to behold.

There were Chinooks, Apaches, Iroquois, Kiowa, Chickasaw . . .

Yes, the themed fancy dress parties were brilliant as well.

# Chapter 29

When I reached Dwyer Base, it was a bleak outpost in the middle of nowhere.

All of a sudden I was surrounded by sandy-headed young men in combat fatigues. I felt at home like never before.

The sand was impossible to avoid. It was as fine as dust, and it was everywhere. It drove you mad.

I stood in front of the window and looked out.

Sand – endless sand. Nothing but sand.

A million billion trillion grains, shifting constantly. A kind of hypnotic beige noise.

It made you think of eternity, of loneliness, of the hugeness of the universe, and one's meaninglessness within it. Humbling, I thought. It sent me spiralling into a philosophical reverie that I felt might have no end.

Did it matter if it didn't end?

Perhaps this was the universe telling me not to worry, and just to think about what mattered. I wondered if this was the case. Thoughtful of it to give me this personal instruction, if so.

'You alright, Harry?' asked my commanding officer.

'Hmm?' I asked, spinning round.

'It's just that you've been staring at that corkboard for forty-five minutes straight.'

'Ah!' I said.

'The window's over there.'

'*Ahh*,' I said, looking out of it.

Behind a burnt-out truck and a sagging pile of sandbags was a bustling outlet of Kandahar Fried Chicken and, in the middle distance, a baby goat chewing a twig.

'Much better view,' I said.

'You sure you're okay, Wales?' he asked.

'Oh, yes. Yes. Of course I am. Look at that little goat, what a sweetie, ha ha,' I said.

# Chapter 30

Once I had settled in at Dwyer Base, it was down to work.

My task was to control messages and send information out to different helicopter teams. It all seemed fearfully technical.

But soon they introduced me to the machine I would be working on.

'Thank god, at last,' I said. 'I'm sick of being thought of as the thicko royal. I'm absolutely dead set on getting stuck in to some serious technical hardware. Really prove those folks wrong!'

'Absolutely,' my commanding officer said. 'Follow me . . .'

The machine I had been assigned to was a device that took in all the information from the many forces in the area, plotted and followed aerial trajectories, and condensed the available intel so that we could relay it to the various teams out there, enabling us to fight the most technologically advanced war ever known in a formidably complex arena.

Yet the machine was deceptively simple. As it was received, all of the input data came out on the screen in a square grid, with different shapes in formations of four blocks descending down the screen.

As each block arrived I had to try and rearrange it to make it fit in with the data blocks already embedded underneath. Once one had made a complete line of data, it was resolved and vanished.

It was a surprisingly challenging but satisfying task.

Sometimes one could not fit the blocks together to resolve the data streams, and they gathered one on the other, with pesky gaps that were annoyingly difficult to eradicate until one had cleared the lines above.

'Well done, Lieutenant Wales,' said my commanding officer, leaning over my shoulder and taking a look at my progress.

Before I could thank him, he turned to where the other soldiers in the same room were playing some video game. They really took it terribly seriously, and were very earnest about the whole exercise. There was lots of urgent shouting and radio communication, presumably with other players at other bases.

But, needing to concentrate on my crucial task, I paid them no heed.

In truth I thought it was somewhat inappropriate for soldiers to be playing a video game in the same room as I was handling crucial life-saving manoeuvres, but I was too junior to consider saying so to my superior officer.

And there was no time anyway – new blocks kept appearing at the top of the screen, and had to be managed. I always had stress-sweat beading on my brow, and at the end of each shift I was so exhausted I flopped into bed and welcoming oblivion.

And protocol is protocol. One doesn't question the chain of command.

I was happy just to be doing a useful job on the dangerous frontier.

# Chapter 31

There was a pole in the middle of the camp, to which soldiers had affixed signs pointing to home.

'Medicine Hat, Saskatchewan – 6,630 miles,' read one.

'Gooloogong, New South Wales – 7,002 miles,' read another.

'Mucky Gooch, Louisiana – 7,415 miles,' said a third.

I reflected for a moment how funny it would be if I put up a sign saying, 'Clarence House – 3,509 miles'. Everyone would laugh and think I was great.

But no, I decided not to. On reflection it would make me look like a massive wanker.

Nevertheless it made me reflect on distances.

In my family, everything was distant.

Or rather, distance was everything.

There was a total lack of physical contact. Famously, my mother had once tried to hug my grandmother, who slid out of the embrace with the whippet-like swiftness of a fly-half.

No one ever hugged, nor even patted each other encouragingly on the shoulder.

We were chronically distant from each other.

And how surprising was it, therefore, that when given the chance I had travelled into the unmappable regions of Afghanistan (and would later leap at opportunities to visit the

North and South Poles), putting all distance possible between us, in order to find myself? Was it natural, or unnatural?

At a royal dinner even the distance of soup bowls within dinner mats was calculated precisely – with tape measures!

Who was in the soup now?

I was.

You can be sure of that. But how far distant into the soup? That, as yet, could not be measured.

# Chapter 32

After several months on the tetra-forming puzzle computer (those shapes never did stop falling – it really made one dizzy to imagine the amount of data being constantly crunched by those massive computers), I graduated to working on the radio.

Now I was managing the airspace and directing the various allied copters and craft that zoomed through it on an hourly basis.

This meant that I had to speak to people from all over the world.

'Hello,' came a voice over the radio from one low-flying helicopter.

'Hi there, can you read me?' I replied.

'Yes I can,' came the response. It was in an American accent. I could tell we were already firm mates.

In warfare, friendships form quickly under intense combat conditions. I knew this was one.

'You have permission to proceed,' I said.

'Bravo,' came the response.

Bravo, indeed! What pals we were! What repartee!

'Keep up the good work dude!' I yelled, punching the air.

There was no response. They must have been out of radio distance by then.

Later that day I met another red-haired soldier, a fellow member of the elite ginger corps. I felt we had a natural chemistry.

He was an Irishman and I gave him a jolly good ribbing about the history between my family and his nation. His eyes twinkled and I could tell straight away we were firm friends.

'Why don't you go and feck yourself,' he said, and spat on my shoes.

I never spoke to him again but knew we were true chums. Bonded by our mutual combat experience.

After all, that was the kind of camaraderie you got in the army.

Dark humour? Hell, yes. That's what we were all about.

I chortled as I wiped his flob off my boot, and heard him swearing loudly as he retreated through the camp telling everyone I was a tosser.

What a guy!

# Chapter 33

It was a quiet night on the radio.

Just sand dunes and moonlight and silence. And one's own thoughts – about sand, and Sandhurst, and Sandringham, and the grains ever trickling through the sandglass of eternity.

Silence, broken by bursts of crackling radio.

Urgent requests, demands for intel.

Then a voice rang out, requesting information on nearby Taliban sightings. It was a female pilot's voice.

We chatted for a few moments, then the airwaves were filled with catcalls from the other military personnel listening in. They told us two to 'get a room'.

It was enjoyable talking to this young female but then suddenly I had visions of what her life would be like if anyone got wind of this and discovered both our identities.

She could be hounded by the press, possibly losing her job and her sanity, driven into hiding. It was an appalling prospect.

'Listen, er, I think we should keep this professional,' I stuttered, Hugh Grant-like, into the microphone.

'Pardon, Hedgehog 7?' she said back.

Hedgehog 7 was my radio call signal. When I had first heard it I knew it was another message from the universe.

That damn universe, with its perverse sense of humour!

55

It was the hedgehog I had seen that night when I was at Eton, calling to me again. Wrinkling its enigmatic nose and shuffling its spiky little bottom, telling me that all would be well.

'I just think we shouldn't let things move too fast,' I stammered. 'I think you're a great girl and all that, please don't misunderstand me . . .'

'Please repeat, Hedgehog 7,' she said. 'I'm not receiving you. I just need directions on where to land and deliver these crates of lavatory disinfectant.'

Atta girl! Pretend that there was nothing between us. Move on with your life. That's the way to play it! I punched the air again.

We never spoke after that, but I always felt there really had been a spark between us.

# Chapter 34

After months out there, near the very epicentre of the war, I was finally face to face with pure evil.

My blood ran cold.

One is trained to face the enemy, rigorously prepared to understand their manoeuvres, their techniques, how they undermine and destroy.

Yet when one is confronted with the reality, one calls on one's deepest resources to stay calm, and act sensibly to protect oneself and the ones one cares about.

The journalist had been invited in by the top brass to watch along as I performed my duties. He was one of a swarm of the creatures who had gathered, insect-like, as soon as they were given the opportunity. Every moment I was in their presence I felt like there were maggots crawling over my skin.

Every move I made, I was under extreme scrutiny, with danger in the tiniest error that might cascade into a life-threatening shit-storm.

I called on all my resources and held it together. The presence of the enemy was a burden I had to outlast.

Finally the assault was over, and with the pre-agreed press tour over, the horde of journalists withdrew.

I felt I could let out a deep breath, relax at last, and return to facing the Taliban.

# Chapter 35

I had completed two tours in a combat zone. Now it was time to go home.

When we left the airbase at Afghanistan, however, we were sent to a secret location for a compulsory week's 'decompression'.

All around, soldiers wandered aimlessly.

Many of us were confused, angry – or not even sure what we were feeling.

A comedy gig was laid on, and we were all expected to attend.

Hardly anyone laughed at a single joke.

I felt bad for the poor comedian, sent all the way out to the Middle East to do surely one of the toughest gigs on the planet.

I watched as this performer energetically goofed around and tried to entertain in front of a phalanx of stony-faced strangers who simply watched his antics pitilessly, refusing to give the smallest sign of approval.

I had absolutely no idea whatsoever how he could possibly be feeling.

# Chapter 36

Back in Britain after Afghanistan, I was a lost soul.

I felt anxious at public events, frequently having panic attacks.

Like many a young man, I self-medicated. I was papped constantly going into or coming out of nightclubs, associating with models.

To avoid photographers, I had my bodyguard pack me into the boot of his car. It was a weird feeling. I don't know what it was about being the family 'spare' that gave me the idea of hiding in there.

At that time I felt I had only a few best friends I could count on.

They were called Whisky and Gin. Vodka and Rum. Southern Comfort and Sambuca.

Funny names for corgis, I thought. But perhaps Grannie had named them to bring back memories of her dear mother.

Either way, at least with the dogs I found unquestioning friendliness.

# Chapter 37

It was a themed fancy dress party, and my presence was mandatory – the theme was Tribes and Colonisers.

I didn't have a costume but at the last minute discovered a hire place near to the party venue. I went, very reluctantly, and practically without thinking about it, almost at random and with my eyes averted, plucked the first outfit that came to hand, and ended up with a Nazi uniform.

Willy and Kate were there and it was probably their idea, to be honest, I really can't quite recall.

In fact, yes, I *can* recall and it definitely *was* their idea.

When the story came out that I had attended a party dressed as a Nazi, it provoked a worldwide scandal.

*Harry the racist, Harry the thicko*, were the headlines.

I couldn't believe I had been so stupid.

What had I been thinking?

I vowed never, ever, to bring the family into disrepute ever again.

# Chapter 38

My mates had somehow talked me into going to Vegas.

I didn't fancy it at all.

Spending all that time in giant, ludicrously expensive and gaudy palaces filled with inane chatter and wasted money? No thanks.

It just wasn't me.

But nonetheless, I caved in at last.

One night we found ourselves playing pool with a band of attractive female croupiers. I suggested that we make the game interesting and play strip pool.

Within minutes I was utterly nude. It was all just a bit of fun, and there was lots of guffawing and backslapping (as well as nadger-clutching).

Next day, the pictures were all over the world. It was a giant scandal.

*Harry the nudist, Harry the thicko, A right royal idiot,* said the headlines.

I couldn't believe I had been so stupid.

What had I been thinking?

I vowed never, ever, to bring the family into disrepute ever again.

After all, if one could not count on honour among scantily clad Las Vegas croupiers, what had happened to the world?

# Chapter 39

With the Vegas story all over the world's press and my cheeks still burning with shame, I cringed at what my army bosses would say when I returned.

I expected to be frogmarched out of the army at once and have my military decorations (orienteering – silver badge, metalwork – bronze badge) ceremonially ripped from my chest.

However, to my surprise they didn't care one jot.

As far as they were concerned, when I was away from duty I was a private citizen and they didn't mind what I did.

It turned out the real reason was that I was already a poster boy for the armed services, and that by signing up, I had drawn thousands of other equally emotionally and psychologically damaged young men and women to join the services.

So they were delighted with me.

Hurray!

# Chapter 40

To clear my head, I had gone again to Botswana, the place where I felt most myself.

It was essential to escape the atrocious press intrusion, which had become unbearable.

With friends, I travelled deep into the wildlands.

We were part of a film crew dedicated to finding various rare animals across the African veldt. Once we had located them, we stalked them carefully and documented their every movement with cutting-edge cameras. We had to attach tracking devices on them so we could trace their migrations with precision.

Once we'd recorded the footage, it would end up on a David Attenborough documentary for millions to enjoy.

We approached one family of snoring black rhinoceroses as quietly as we could.

Then there was the snap of a twig.

We swivelled, to find a pack of paparazzi a hundred feet away, pointing at us with their cameras, which were adorned with three-foot-long telephoto lenses.

How they had found us, we couldn't imagine.

Later, while enjoying the documentary on television, we discovered that there had been a small electronic device hidden on our car telling them where we were to be found at all times.

Just so they could record us and then sell the footage for public consumption.

Such despicable intrusion.

The hypocrisy of the paps was galling.

# Chapter 41

On our lads' holiday through America, we stopped in Tennessee to visit the house of the King.

'I thought America didn't do kings?' I joshed. Everyone laughed and thought I was brilliant.

Seriously, though, this king lived in Memphis – named after the ancient Egyptian capital. So perhaps he should have been called the Pharaoh of Rock?

That made me think of sand again. Sand, endless sand, pouring one grain over the other ... the meaninglessness of it, the impersonal wonder of the echoing space in the desert ...

Then a friend poked me in the ribs and told me to quit staring at a corkboard on the wall.

'Oh, ah,' I said, snapping out of it. 'I was thinking. Shouldn't they have made him the President of Rock and Roll? Or better still, if they're interested in having a king, it's well known I'm going spare.'

But then, I imagined the Americans being stuck with an immature red-haired leader, who caused ceaseless controversial headlines, and fought an endless battle with the media.

They wouldn't stand for that.

The more I learned about Elvis, the more I felt a complex connection with him. He was very close to his mother, which I could quite understand, and he was bereft after her passing. In fact it seemed to cause him significant psychological damage, affecting his maturity and making him a very troubled adult.

But for him to write and release 'Oliver's Army', celebrating the roundheads in the English Civil War?

No, thank you.

That put him quite beyond the pale.

I took *off* my blue suede shoes – I felt no high fidelity to this recording artist! And as to his early death due to barbiturate abuse, well, accidents will happen. I decided to turn off the radio, radio.

Though at that time I *did* want to go to Chelsy (my then girl-friend). She had me all shook up, and was this year's model. We couldn't help falling in love, and casting complicated shadows.

Chelsy and I would soon have our final tryst, however, at Heartbreak Hotel. After which, I would be shipbuilding, to sail away, singing: please release me.

O-bla-di, O-bla-da.

# Chapter 42

At the wedding I was delighted to watch my dear friend get hitched.

At the end of the night, however, when all couples had paired off and I was still alone, I couldn't help feeling bitter. When was I going to meet my perfect partner?

What did the universe have against me?

Damn universe, I thought. Give me a break, why can't you?

The universe certainly had a mean sense of humour. I felt as though it was flipping me off, or possibly holding out a fist, and then with its other hand winding an invisible crank, so that its middle finger slowly rose in a disrespectful salute, as though via a mechanical winch.

Universe, I thought, are you gaslighting me?

These days, I feel, the universe's behaviour back then would have been seen as problematic.

Perhaps it would even get cancelled.

However, at that moment the only thing that seemed to have been cancelled was my own future happiness.

# Chapter 43

I had been on a trek to the North Pole to raise money for charity.

However, a few days after I got home, I discovered something was badly wrong. Wrong, that is, with my *south* pole.

I had frost-nip on my royal todge.

How embarrassing – and worse, how to find a physician to treat it? I didn't even know how to phrase the question.

But something had to give – it was agonising!

After some carefully phrased enquiries, at last I found myself being ushered in through the back entrance of a Harley Street practice.

The doctor didn't look up from his desk as I came in, but told me to disrobe. I did so, and there was an uncomfortably long pause while he finished the notes he was working on.

He came behind the curtain and saw me for the first time.

'What an over-sensitive dick,' he said.

I was grateful to be in the hands of someone who could make such a rapid diagnosis.

# Chapter 44

I had returned from my trek to the North Pole just in time to attend Willy's wedding.

It was, of course, a grand affair.

In accordance with tradition, we were both required to wear strange military uniforms with which we were unacquainted. We didn't like them – mine, especially, felt very unflattering and alien to me. I was stuck with it, though. It was the required regimental dress, on such an occasion, for the third in line to the throne.

There was another ceremonial position the press had reported that I was to hold that day – that of being Willy's best man.

As so often, the newspapers were wrong in this.

I was speechless.

Literally. Because best-man duty was given to two great pals of Willy's, who carried it off with aplomb.

Even though I would have been the obvious choice for the role, for some reason Willy and the family had baulked at the idea of allowing me to perform a best man's speech.

They were afraid that if given an opportunity to embarrass the family, I would have made lots of very shameful remarks that would have put them all in a humiliating light.

I could not understand why.

Anyway, at this time my penis (which is circumcised by the way) was still in a lot of pain.

# Chapter 45

Not long after completing my second tour of duty, I was invited to go to the South Pole.

I wasn't sure if I would be up to the challenge.

Once we touched down on the Antarctic and I climbed down and looked around, my soul felt alive. I did a handstand from sheer glee.

I was in a place of extreme coldness and emotional distance, with the only distraction from the arid emptiness being white powder.

I immediately felt at home.

# Chapter 46

I had come across this utterly wonderful woman on a friend's Instagram post. We had been given each other's numbers, and had been texting each other like crazy.

Now it was time to meet.

But where? Of course, going to a regular restaurant was out of the question.

'Join me at Soho House, 76 Dean Street,' she said.

'Okay,' I replied.

'It's great here, they love me.'

We agreed to meet in a private dining room.

I thought this girl was dynamite. I couldn't wait.

But before I could reach our rendezvous at Soho House, I had to get through the traffic. It was at a standstill.

Like my heart.

It was impossible for me just to hop out and run along the street – that would be making a spectacle of myself. And I couldn't imagine ever doing that.

I texted her: 'Running late – so sorry!'

My car was crammed in the centre of an unmoving mass of black cabs and red buses at Piccadilly. The statue of Eros pointed his arrow mockingly over the roof of my car.

I was terribly afraid that Meghan would lose heart, and leave.

That I would arrive only to be presented with the sight of an empty chair.

'Nearly here yet?' she texted back.

As the traffic crawled forward around Britain's most notoriously busy thoroughfare I tried to think of a good way of contextualising how bad the congestion had been, to a foreigner who might not understand London traffic issues.

At last, my car got there. I leapt up the stairs into the private room at Soho House, 76 Dean Street.

She was still sat at the table.

She smiled up at me.

'It was like Regent Street out there!' I said.

We met eyes and smiled.

I had sprinted up the stairs. I was breathing hard.

'I *love* breathing!' she said. 'We have so much in common!'

It turned out that we had the same favourite food.

Chicken.

When we found this out, we stared at each other, open-mouthed.

This was meant to be!

Needless to say, the first date went brilliantly.

# Chapter 47

She was even more ravishing in person than she had seemed from her pictures. I couldn't believe my eyes.

What was best about her was that she couldn't care twopence that I was a royal. It was perfect.

'I hear that you are in the hit US TV drama *Suits*,' I said.

'It's a seemingly never-ending soap opera about tiresome, privileged people bitching, manipulating and betraying each other for power,' she replied.

'Let's not talk about my family,' I said. 'Tell me about *Suits* . . .'

# Chapter 48

We knew we had to meet up again – and as soon as possible.

But how was I, a fully employed member of the Royal Family, going to be able to find a hole in my schedule that matched that of an actor in a major American TV series?

We opened our diaries and compared dates.

'This summer is particularly difficult,' she said, 'because I'm going travelling. Doing the whole *Eat, Pray, Love* thing.'

Eat, pray, love?

What now?

I stared at her. She explained it was a three-leg holiday with her girl chums, taking in Italy, Spain and India.

'That's amazing,' I said. 'I've got a three-leg lads' holiday booked. We're calling it the "Drink, Snort, Vom" tour.'

Her eyes sparkled.

We were made for each other.

# Chapter 49

The first date with Meghan had been a stunning success, and I was elated. However, before the second date could come round, I had to go on a trip.

It was a boat race across the open ocean.

My heart raced, my mind was in a whirl. My life had changed for ever now I had met this wonderful woman, I knew that.

Would I be up to the challenge? Would we survive the tribulations that family life would bring? Did I have the courage?

Once at sea, we got into stormy weather. Heavy winds were battering us from every side.

With the swell at its highest I suddenly found I needed the toilet, but when it came to relieving myself over the side of the boat, my nerve failed. So I did it in my pants.

After I told him this, my ghost-writer said he had to pour himself a drink and go and lie down for a bit.

He complained of something he called 'metaphor fatigue'.

# Chapter 50

Meghan and I were popping round to see my aunt Sarah Ferguson.

I was looking forward to introducing the Duchess of York to the new woman in my life, when I saw an unexpected car in the driveway and extra armed guards by the door.

I wondered what was up – and then my aunt came rushing out to meet us. My worst fears were confirmed.

Grannie was visiting.

Aunty Sarah and I always had an affinity. After all, we are literally ginger royalty. Along with Ginger Spice's Union Jack mini dress, I suppose. It was always nice to see her, but right now we had a problem.

Meghan had to be told how to address the Queen in ten seconds flat. She performed a curtsey with aplomb after being shown how, and rehearsed the correct form of address.

'You call her "Your Majesty" the first time, and afterwards "ma'am" to rhyme with "spam".'

She repeated it perfectly – and a few minutes later, when introduced to Grannie, did so again. All had gone off without a hitch, and in fact Grannie seemed instantly to warm to my beloved.

Sarah and I wiped nervous sweat from our brows.

We had been horrified that Meghan would try to high-five the monarch, or grab her in a bear hug, give her a chest-bump, or flip the Maj over her shoulder in a friendly fireman's lift, all spirited high-jinks we were sure were common among Americans.

'Well done,' I said to Meghan afterwards.

'I don't know what you were worried about,' she told me. 'You see potential disasters everywhere! You are always paranoid about scandal breaking out!'

I admitted this was true. It was quite worrying being a royal, after all, with the potential for controversy lurking at every corner, threatening to bring the family into disrepute.

'What is the name of the queen's assistant, who held her bag?' Meghan asked.

'Not an assistant – that's my uncle Andrew,' I replied cheerfully. 'We certainly don't need to worry about him!'

# Chapter 51

Meghan and I needed some time together to get to know each other.

We flew to my favourite place in the whole world, Botswana. Or Botty, as I like to call it.

The whole trip was perfect. A tonic. The lush Okavango Delta was filled with rainwater at this time of year and had exploded into life.

Just as my heart was filling, with love.

Meghan cooed and yelped in delight as the jeep drove past wonderful sights on every side.

A pair of elephants, mating.

Two giraffes, getting it on.

A couple of crocodiles, knocking boots.

Impalas impaling each other.

'It's just so full of life, and love,' she said, staring deeply into my eyes.

At night we lay side by side listening to the animals on the plain outside, as they came near to the tent.

'I can see you love Africa,' she said.

'I do,' I agreed. 'There's something about seeing these majestic beasts ripping each other to shreds and fighting over corpses that just reminds me of home.'

The whole week-long trip was just what we both needed: a marvellous piece of Botty fun.

# Chapter 52

The news of our relationship had broken. It was in all the papers.

The next day Meghan was in a local supermarket, gathering ingredients for a special dinner, when she was harassed and persecuted by a sequence of aggressive men.

They followed her down the street, shouting ('Give us a smile!') and taking photos of her all the way. Obnoxious, intrusive, inhuman, cruel.

When I found her, she was in tears.

I was so sorry. I had promised to protect her, and had failed.

All her friends were asking, was it worth it to go through this, just to be with me? Even I wasn't sure that I knew the answer to that one.

I hugged her tight, said consoling words, and kissed her.

I couldn't believe my ears.

Then I couldn't believe my nostrils.

'You still made dinner, after all that?' I asked.

She had – a gammon joint.

'How did you do it?' I asked. 'I'm absolutely useless at cooking. Tell me the process?'

'Take this innocent lump of meat,' she explained, 'plunge it in hot water and turn the heat up.'

'Then?'

'Beware the scum that rises to the surface,' she said.
'You don't have to tell me,' I replied.
It turns out I did understand the basics of cooking after all.

# Chapter 53

Pa approached Willy and me to ask our approval for him and Camilla to get married.

We had begged him not to. We feared the press interest it would stir up about our collective past.

But he was intent upon it. And seeing the happiness it would give him, we didn't hesitate to give our blessing.

The date was fixed for Windsor Castle.

Then, all of a sudden, the Pope died.

And the wedding was immediately postponed.

What now?

Really?

How did that matter?

It seemed that the Pope's funeral was going to be held the same weekend as Pa and Camilla's proposed wedding.

My father and his bride-to-be couldn't possibly allow the attention to be taken away from their special day.

The occasion when a new future head of state would suddenly take the place of a worshipped deceased predecessor could not be made to clash with the Pope's funeral.

I was secretly relieved.

I couldn't help feeling that perhaps it was my mother,

somewhere in the universe, helping to postpone something she didn't approve of.

How exactly she had managed it from the grave, I wasn't quite sure.

When she had learned the date Pa and Camilla intended to marry, she must have travelled to Rome to kill the elderly Pope at a time carefully calibrated to produce a funeral that coincided with the planned nuptials.

I didn't know whether or how exactly ghosts could travel, whether they had to go to an airport and get on a plane, or otherwise walk all the way to the destination including going across the bottom of the English Channel and coming out at Calais or Cherbourg.

Possibly – more likely perhaps – they could just blip where they wanted to by exercising some ghostly teleportation ability.

Once in Rome, of course, one would have to find the Vatican apartments and then perform such ghostly activities as would speed the death of a frail Pope.

But what if, on arrival, one found the pontiff fading faster than expected? Then she would somehow have to artificially *extend* his life, via whatever means available to her, till the right moment.

All in all, it would take a considerable amount of ghostly planning. But then she was always a perfectionist.

As I stared up at the stars, I breathed in the night air.

I felt the scenario I had come up with was probably what had happened.

Then I was startled out of my reverie by a noise.

It was Meghan calling down to me from the bedroom window to put my joint out and come to bed.

# Chapter 54

I decided that it was time to pop the question with Meghan.

To my amazement I was told I had to ask Grannie's permission before proposing. Really?

Well, yes.

But really though??

Yes! Stop saying really!

I picked my moment carefully. One rarely gets a chance to be alone with Grannie.

It was on a hunting afternoon at Balmoral that I finally saw my chance. I pounced.

I utterly loved Grannie, but she could be a difficult person to read. Very subtle in her facial expressions, with her mysterious little smiles and understated humour. I knew that she was fond of me, but couldn't be *quite* sure what she thought of me and my chosen partner, as a couple.

All of a sudden we were alone in a field, dogs running around us merrily. Wisps of fog drifted across the moor.

I was short of words, my mouth was dry. But eventually I got it out.

' . . . so you see, I have to ask your permission, Grannie. May I have it?'

She glanced at me with a twinkle in her eyes, and an

unreadable expression. For a moment my whole universe stopped moving. I couldn't breathe.

Finally she picked her nose, flicked the bogey away and in the distinctive cockney bass, which is her true voice when she's away from the cameras, said: 'Fill yer facking boots, 'arry. See if I give two shits.' And let out a burp that would shatter bone china from the opposite side of a football pitch.

Then she turned away, calling the dogs after her.

# Chapter 55

I had found myself staying temporarily at Courtney Cox's house, and there was a party.

It was a relief to be among celebrities, because they had fundamentally similar lives to mine, and understood the pressures. For instance, of not being always 'on' and also allowing one to be a different person when away from public scrutiny to the person one had to be when in the glare of the spotlight.

To escape from the constant barrage of identical questions, the demands to perform like a puppet. Asked the same thing thoughtlessly, over and again.

Then I found out that the actor playing Batman was at the party.

'Do the Batman voice!' I yelled.

He sighed and looked irritated but, after a pause, complied with my request.

'That's amazing!' I said. 'That's so cool! Do it again!'

He looked at me like I was joking for a moment, but then seeing that I wasn't, with deep reluctance, did it again.

'I'm talking to Batman! I can't believe it!' I chirruped. 'Do it again!'

But at that moment someone else seemed to catch his eye and he darted off.

How great it was to be able to relax around people who really understood one.

# Chapter 56

In recent times I had begun experimenting with hallucinogens. First for fun, then for their therapeutic value.

I happened to take a dose with a friend while I was at the party at Courtney Cox's house.

After a while I could feel the effects starting, so I excused myself to the bathroom, to take a moment's privacy.

'Hello, Harry,' said the toilet.

'What? Are you talking to me? Really?'

'I am,' said the toilet. 'What do you want to know?'

'I want to know why everyone is so hard on me, Mr Toilet,' I said.

'Please, Harry,' said the toilet. 'Mr Toilet is my father, you can call me Loo.'

'Ah, right.'

'That's just a piece of toilet humour right there,' said the toilet.

'I can't believe this is happening,' I said.

'Well, it isn't. But try to enjoy it anyway. My answer to your question though, Harry, is that you ignored all the advice of your family members and engaged with the press. They were intrusive, of course they were, and their behaviour was undoubtedly disgusting.

'But as you admit, your own father had suffered very similar

press intrusion when he was a young man and by sticking to his guns he pulled through and played the long game.

'Those older and wiser than you told you to keep your mouth shut and it would blow over. But you showed anger, and that just encouraged the press. They smelled blood, and now they'll never leave you alone, you see? It's a real shame the way things have shaken out, and hopefully in the long term you'll be able to reconnect with your family. Also, what's this thing where you keep mentioning the London address of Soho House? Have you got a product placement deal with them or something?'

The toilet sighed. 'Your main problem – it seems to me – is that you're basically a nice average guy, stuck in an extraordinary situation. But also, kind of a whiny navel-gazing millennial.'

'What do you know?' I said to him. 'You're full of shit.'

'Well, that's true as well,' he admitted. 'Now go out there and enjoy the party. You're in Courtney Cox's house, for god's sake!'

I left the loo and told my friend (who had also taken a dose) that he *had* to go into the toilet because it was the experience of a lifetime. To my frustration my friend would never stop talking long enough for me to get a word in edgeways.

Then Courtney Cox appeared.

'Harry?' she said. 'Why are you talking to that wall mirror?'

# Chapter 57

When the time came close for our wedding, there were of course certain important formal rituals to be observed.

First and foremost was a stag do.

I can't quite recall the thoughtful planning and conversations that preceded it. But all of a sudden there I was, dressed as a chicken, having fireworks aimed at me by a bunch of drunk aristocrats.

It was incredibly moving.

The chicken costume, of course, represented Meghan's and my shared favourite food. Chicken. I still could hardly believe people from such different backgrounds shared such eclectic taste.

The fireworks represented the explosions of love and bright shining sparks of happiness that had gone off in both our lives since we had met.

Most of all, however, it was deeply moving because it's so hard to get out of the way of a flaming missile shooting towards your nether regions when you're dressed in a chicken costume.

My desperate manoeuvres on the firing range that day also represented the energy with which I would protect the particular feast – the roast chicken dinner – that Meghan and I had chosen to make of our lives together.

And the increasingly singed feathers told of the desperation we would both feel as the supposedly joyful fireworks of marital bliss turned into blistering infernos of hate and unwelcome press intention.

Why did the chicken cross the pond?

To escape getting a horrible firework up his arse, that's why.

# Chapter 58

There were difficulties between us and our wives. Sometimes we were at each other's throats.

And yet there were moments of communion and tenderness between Willy and me. He was under the same pressures as I was, being briefed against by Charles and Camilla.

Sometimes we would go for walks in the Palace grounds and share our frustrations. Our doubts.

One time I admitted to him that I felt our mother was still out there, watching over us. I felt vulnerable saying it, feeling he might mock me.

But he said he felt it too.

'She's there, Willy, guiding us. Helping us. I feel it.'

He agreed.

'I think she helped me find Meghan, too,' I said.

'No, Harry,' he said. 'That's just bollocks.'

# Chapter 59

Times were getting tough, and tensions building in the royal family. I was sure that various factions – Pa and Camilla, Willy and Kate – were constantly briefing the press against Meghan and me.

The pressure began to grow unbearable.

Newspapers would describe Kate closing a car door in a manner heroic, brave, beautiful and regal. The next day, Meghan performing the exact same innocuous action would be described as venomous, aggressive, presumptuous and vulgar.

There were constant stories in the press about Meghan behaving with 'abrasive cheerfulness', 'arrogant friendliness' and 'sly competence' as well as accusing her of 'vicious generosity'. There were also reports that her breathing was coarse.

It was impossible.

The time had come. We had to leave the country.

# Chapter 60

All I wanted to do was work. To be active. To spread the message.

I had flown around the world on what seemed like a never-ending trip.

I had given talks at stadiums, hospitals, universities. To thousands upon thousands of people.

I had spoken on TV shows, given interviews for news broadcasts and to late-night pundits.

Everything I had done was to raise awareness.

At last I returned home. I was exhausted.

'You've done an amazing job, Harry,' Meghan said at last. 'You have raised worldwide awareness to an unprecedented level.'

'I have?' I asked.

'Yes,' she said.

'Really?' I asked.

'I've told you already to stop saying "really" all the time,' she said. 'My love,' she added quickly.

'I'm glad you think I've sufficiently raised awareness,' I said.

'You have,' she said. 'The entire world definitely now knows that you are incredibly pissed off with your family.'

At last I could relax.

# Chapter 61

It seemed to come out of the blue.

Willy just turned up at my house one day, and said we needed to talk.

As always when we argued, neither of us listened to the other. The row grew fiercer and fiercer until all of a sudden he grabbed my shirt collar and ripped it.

I tottered, fell, and cracked the dog bowl with my back.

He stood over me, breathing hard.

It had never come to this before. It was a new frontier for us as adults, physical battery.

'*I'm* the one who gets to support charities to do with domestic violence,' he roared, snorting with rage. 'Just butt out! I get to support hippos and lions and Africa, too. Find your own bloody little charities to support! Human trafficking or something!'

He was right. After all, I had been human trafficking for a long time – that is, trafficking in human misery. My own misery. Perhaps it was time to offer myself a little charity?

Alas, it was no use crying over spilled milk.

I could not cry, anyway, no more than my uncle Andrew could sweat. As a family we were notorious retainers of liquid.

The liquid that had been spilled this time was the milk of

human kindness. I was afraid that it was curdling – into the yoghurt of human despair.

And I knew for sure it was time Meghan and I trafficked ourselves across the pond – to a new life, and freedom, and a seriously juicy wodge of Netflix moolah.

# Chapter 62

At last, Meghan and I had a family around us, and had made a home that was warm and full of love.

The universe certainly had a funny way of doing things. I was happy, finally.

If I could meet it now, I would give the universe a high-five, and maybe drink a tequila with it.

'You're a cracking universe after all,' I would say, giving it a hug and perhaps putting my arm round its neck to give it a boisterous noogie into the bargain. The universe would laugh along with me.

We'd be great pals. 'Maybe there are better universes out there, but I can't imagine one!' I'd chortle. 'For my money, you're the best universe in the ... well, the world!'

When I was around Meghan, I felt like the cat who had got a great big serving of the *cream* of human kindness. And at long last I was starting to feel that together we might churn it into the butter of domestic bliss.

Vegan butter, of course.

For our new life was to be in California. Where famous people are allowed to live in peace, and not mercilessly ripped to shreds and then dispensed with by a shallow, fast-churning media cycle. Certainly not!

Plus, weed is legal here.

So this particular royal weed, having plucked himself out of the poisoned regal rose garden, will replant himself again, and grow.

With his little family buds growing off his main shoot, adoring the life-giving Californian sun ... the rich, fecund soil ... ripe tomatoes on the vine ... cilantro ... arugula ...

Shit, I could kill a burrito right now.

What was I thinking about again?

Yes, Meghan! I've put it out! Coming!